GAME ON NORTHUMBERLAND

FAVOURITE GAME RECIPES FROM THE HEART OF NORTHUMBERLAND

EMMA WHITTINGHAM

Game On Press

First published in Great Britain in 2011 by Game On Press

Copyright © Emma Whittingham, 2011

A CIP catalogue record for this book is available from the British Library

ISBN 978-0-9570160-0-2

Designed by Luminous Creative, Edinburgh
Printed in Great Britain by Martins the Printers Ltd,
Berwick-upon-Tweed, Northumberland

HEALTHY EATING DOESN'T HAVE TO BE BORING OR DULL, no matter what people might think. It can be fun and exciting, as well as being good for you. If you're going to draw inspiration for healthy eating from anywhere, the British countryside is the best place to start. With everything to choose from; from button mushrooms and floury potatoes to succulent, juicy apples, why look anywhere else? There is nothing more enticing than strawberries freshly picked from the fields, or the mouthwatering smell of slow roasted venison. Hunting wild game goes far beyond it being a wild sport. It is a means for securing lean, nutritious meat, which are excellent sources of protein, generally containing less fat.

If you're unsure where to start, this recipe book will equip you with everything you need to turn local produce into creative, culinary masterpieces.

BON APPÉTIT

A BIENTÔT

JEAN CHRISTOPHE NOVELLI

WITH THANKS TO

www.alnwickfoodfestival.co.uk

THE NORTHUMBERLAND ESTATES

INTRODUCTION

Northumberland is a boon for foodies. Some of the best food in the world is on our doorstep—seasonal game such as prize venison and rabbit as well as a wide variety of fresh local produce.

Part of our heritage is the recipes that have been handed down through generations, and our legacy is what we pass on. This book is the culmination of my favourite recipes gathered from our community of local 'experts'.

I hope my wee book will inspire your palettes and encourage not just the use of local Game but all local produce.

Let's keep it Local.

Emma Whittingham

Thanks to Theo, Henz, my amazing parents, family and friends. Thanks to James Chapple Properties and Barter Books for their inspiration and encouragement.

CONTENTS

PHEASANT

ASSORTED GAME BIRDS

RABBIT

PHEASANT

PHEASANT

PHEASANT BREASTS WITH MUSHROOM & THYME SAUCE BY JUDITH HODGSON (Serves 4)

6 pheasant breasts
1 tbsp. olive oil
1 tbsp. redcurrant jelly
50g butter
225g small brown mushrooms (quartered)
1 small leek finely sliced
40g flour
450ml hot game stock
100ml dry sherry
1 tbsp. thyme leaves (chopped)
1–2 tbsp. double cream

Heat oil in a frying pan and brown the breasts briefly on each side. Remove from pan and set aside. Melt butter, add leaks and mushrooms then fry over a high heat until soft. Blend in the flour and gradually add the stock and sherry, stirring until blended and bring to boil. Add redcurrant jelly, chopped thyme and cream. Season with salt and pepper and return breasts to pan. Bring to boil, cover and simmer over a low heat for 35 minutes until breasts are tender.

Judith Hodgson is a talented lady. Not only does she run an elegant bed and breakfast in Tillmouth, she is a full-on mum and still finds the time to cook and bake like a dream. It was Judith's husband Noel, a well-known local poet, who first encouraged and inspired me to create this book.

OLD ENGLISH GAME STEW BY JANE HALL
(Serves 4)

PHEASANT

1 lb. chuck steak
1 large old pheasant
(I use pheasant breasts and the remainder of the bird for stock)
2 oz. butter
4 large celery sticks (coarsely chopped)
6 oz. onion (finely sliced)
3 level tbsp. plain flour
¼ pint Port
¾ pint light stock
Salt and milled pepper

Forcemeat balls
4 oz. streaky bacon
2 oz. onion (finely chopped)
1 oz. butter
4 oz. fresh white breadcrumbs
¼ tsp. dried thyme
1 egg beaten
Snipped parsley

CUT STEAK into 2" x ½" strips. Joint pheasant into 6 pieces, remove
end wing joints, back bone, feathers, etc. Brown steak pieces in hot
fat, then drain and repeat for the pheasant. Add celery and onion until
lightly brown. Stir in flour, port, stock, seasoning and bring to the boil,
stirring. Replace beef and pheasant, cook at 180°C {350°F} for 2 hours.
Meanwhile grill bacon until crisp, remove rind and snip into small
pieces. Add onion and fry until soft, stir in breadcrumbs with bacon,
seasoning and herbs, bind with egg and shape into 6 even sized balls.
Place meat in casserole and cook for a further 30 minutes at 190°C
{375°F}. Adjust seasoning and snip in parsley. This can be frozen for
one month, ideally no more than two.

J ANE is yet another talented Northumbrian Lady. I used this recipe
for a supper party, roaring success.

PHEASANT

MARGARET'S PHEASANT WITH MUSHROOMS (Serves 4)

1 pheasant (drawn and plucked)
1 tbsp. olive oil
2 oz. butter
1 onion chopped
1 shallot chopped
1 carrot chopped
3 ½ oz. cooked ham (diced)
1 fresh rosemary sprig
4 fresh sage leaves chopped
1 bay leaf
1 ¾ pints chicken stock
7 oz. button mushrooms
1 garlic clove
7 oz. stoned green olives
Salt and pepper

Season the cavity of the pheasant with salt and pepper and truss with kitchen string. Heat the olive oil and half the butter in a pan. Add the pheasant and cook, turning frequently until browned all over and then remove from pan. Add the onion, shallot, carrot, ham and herbs to the pan. Season with salt and pepper and pour in the stock. Cover and simmer on a low heat for about 15 minutes. Return the pheasant to the pan, re-cover and simmer for a further 40 minutes. Melt the remaining butter in another pan, adding the mushrooms and garlic to brown and stirring occasionally for about 10 minutes. Remove the mushrooms from the pan, add the olives and cook gently for 5 minutes. Add the olives and mushrooms to the pheasant and cook for a further few minutes. Transfer the bird and vegetables to a warm serving dish after discarding the rosemary, bay leaf and garlic.

Margaret Holt, in my opinion, was one of the best game cooks in Northumberland. Her recipes are creative and delicious.

CHRISTMAS PHEASANT BY HILDA TULIP
(Serves 4–6)

Brace of pheasants {2}
25g butter
2 tbsp. olive oil
4 rashers of smoked bacon

PHEASANT

Stuffing
150g of pork sausage meat
1 onion finely diced
1 leek finely chopped
25g butter
12 tbsp. olive oil
3 rashers of smoked bacon
1 tbsp. thyme
1 tbsp. sage
100g chestnuts

START WITH STUFFING. Sauté onions and leek in butter and olive oil, then add bacon and cook until crispy. Once cooled, add the herbs, chestnuts and sausage meat. No salt is required. Fill the cavity of the birds with the stuffing, then smear with butter and drizzle olive oil. Place the birds on a baking tray and cover the breasts with bacon rashers. Cover with foil and place in oven at 200°C {390°F} or top AGA and roast for 50 minutes. Remove foil and return for a further 20 minutes to crisp.

HILDA CAN COOK! I first met Hilda when I was a child and cherish fond memories of her kind family. Many a time, Hugh Tulip would have a wagon load of ponies and children to take hunting for the day—brave man—and Hilda's soup upon returning was to die for! This recipe is a fantastic alternative to traditional turkey. As a Farmer's Market Trader and Farmer's wife, Hilda knows more than a thing or two about cooking Northumbrian produce.

PHEASANT

PHEASANT BROTH BY EMMA
(Serves 6–8)

2 pheasant carcasses from roast or casserole
2 diced onions
2 leeks finely chopped
2 large carrots grated
200g broth mix
2 chicken stock cubes
Cracked black pepper and sea salt

{Ginger olive oil and Parmesan for serving}

REMOVE ANY MEAT left on the pheasant and place to one side. Put the
carcasses in a large stock pot and cover with water (roughly 4 pints).
Bring to the boil and reduce heat to low for 2 hours. Sieve the stock
and add in the remaining meat from the carcass. Using the same stock
pot, sauté the onions and leeks in olive oil for 10 minutes, then reduce
heat to low, add carrots and broth mix. Pour in the stock and pheasant,
add stock cubes and salt and pepper to taste. I like to leave this on a
low heat for at least 2 hours; it tastes even better the next day.

THIS IS definitely not a starter. Serve with hot bread and
Parmesan. If you can get your hands on Colonna Ginger oil,
even better!

IRENE'S POINT-to-POINT PIE
USING A 27cm (10") x 8cm(3") TIN

1 ½ lb. pheasant meat
3 lbs. ham — soak if salty for a couple of hours

Cook each in foil for 1 hour. Bring out, cool, drain off jelly and put aside. Mince ham and an onion and add:

½ pint milk and 2 eggs
1 tsp. cracked black pepper
1 tsp. Provençal herbs

Line greased tin with pastry made with:
1 lb. plain four
4 ½ oz. lard
4 oz. margarine
1 tsp. salt
NB: Keep ¼ of the pastry for lid

Add, by layers, mince and chicken. Put on lid and decorate with pastry leaves and roses. Cook for 1 hour at 190°C {375°F}. take out of oven and brush with beaten egg and then return to oven for 20 minutes at 180°C {350°F}. Return warmed jelly to pie when cold using funnel.

ANOTHER FAMILY FAVOURITE from my mother.

PHEASANT RESCUE RECIPE BY EMMA
(Serves 6–8)

PHEASANT

Brace of pheasants {2}
Olive oil or Oleifera
3 finely diced onions
3 cloves of crushed garlic
6 oranges
20 small carrots
Stock from pheasant and 1 pint of water
2 chicken stock cubes (optional)
1 bottle of red wine
3 tsp. corn flour
Cracked black pepper and salt

PLACE ONE ORANGE inside the cavity of each bird and massage with oil.
Place birds on a large roasting tin upside down. Cover with foil and
roast on a high heat 220–230°C {425–450°F} for 30 minutes. Reduce
the heat to 180°C and slow roast for a further 1 ½ hours. Once birds
have cooled, remove all the meat. Sieve all the stock from the roasting
pan and put aside. Take a large casserole or soup pan and sauté onions
until brown, then add whole carrots and the juice from the remaining
4 oranges. Add the pheasant meat, pour the stock over and cook on a
high heat for 10 minutes. Add wine, water, stock cubes, corn flour, salt
and pepper. Cook on a low heat for a further 2 hours. Serve with local
mashed potatoes, turnips and haggis.

I DISCOVERED this recipe over ten years ago. One very snowy
winter in Bolton, I found myself snowed in with four guests and
a very hungry young family—what was I to make? Delving into
my freezer, I produced a brace of pheasants and discovered oranges,
potatoes, carrots, onions and a haggis rolling around in my fridge. This
was a challenge I was going to enjoy! It was a success and has become a
family favourite. Total comfort food.

ASSORTED GAME BIRDS

PIGEON RISOTTO BY VICKY GALLON
(Serves 4)

GAME BIRDS

500g risotto rice (roughly one handful per person)
1 litre of chicken stock
Handful of dried wild mushrooms*
2 pigeons
1 large onion (finely chopped)
3 garlic cloves (finely chopped)
½ glass of Madeira wine or sherry
Mushrooms of choice (chestnut preferred)
Peas (fresh or frozen, cooked separately)
2 tbsp. Parmesan

Remove the pigeon breasts and, in a hot pan, fry skin side down for a few minutes to get a good colour on the meat. If you like yours rare, remove from the heat. If not, then pop in the top of the AGA for a further 5 minutes.

Using the same pan, fry the risotto rice in olive oil until the rice begins to turn translucent (approximately 3 minutes), then add the onions, garlic and mushrooms and fry for a further 5 minutes. Splosh in the wine (remembering to take a sip) and stir. Add stock a bit at a time, stirring regularly until stock is gone (tip: don't add more stock until the liquid in the pan is completely absorbed). This will take about 20 minutes. Season to taste, then stir in the peas and the Parmesan. Give your pigeon breasts a final flash in the pan and roughly slice. I like to serve this with some fresh rocket and parsley with a good sized glass of Rioja.

*Reconstitute the mushrooms in water for at least half an hour, drain and add to the stock for extra flavour.

A T ONLY 23 Vicky is one of the most talented chefs in Northumberland. She manages Pilgrims Coffee Shop on Holy Island with Andrew Mundy. Pilgrims goes to great lengths to provide a locally sourced menu and the best coffee to be found in Northumberland.

PIGEON BRUNCH BY PETER GALLON
(Serves 4)

4 pigeon breasts
4 slices of granary bread
2 oz. butter
4 tbsp. olive oil
1 large red onion (finely sliced)
2 beef tomatoes (finely sliced)
Handful of fresh parsley (chopped)
4 handfuls of rocket
Cracked black pepper

GAME BIRDS

Heat the olive oil in a large frying pan and sauté the onions.
Increase the heat and pan fry the pigeon breasts, searing on both sides
for 3 to 4 minutes. Reduce the heat to medium and cook for a further
5 minutes. Cover and remove from heat. Using another frying pan,
heat 2 tablespoons of olive oil and the butter. Once sizzling, fry the
bread on both sides. Place the bread on a plate and start building your
brunch! Arrange tomatoes, topped with a handful of rocket, onions
then pigeon breast. Add a sprinkling of chopped parsley and cracked
black pepper. Wash down with a large mug of coffee.

Vicky's dad often came home with freshly shot wood pigeon
and she looked forward to this delicious brunch. A simple and
satisfying way to serve pigeon.

SLOW ROAST MALLARD BY SALLY BLACK
(Serves 2)

GAME BIRDS

2 mallard
1 tbsp. olive oil
25g butter
5 shallots (diced)
2 cloves of garlic
3 celery sticks (finely diced)
1 orange
1 glass of red wine
1 shot of Cointreau
½ pint of stock
½ tbsp. of flour
Black pepper and salt to season

Put a quarter orange inside each dressed mallard and place in a large roasting tin. Gently melt the butter and pour over the birds, turning them upside down for roasting. Cook at 220°C {425°F} or top AGA for 30 minutes. While the birds are roasting start the sauce. Use a heavy bottom frying pan to heat the olive oil. Add the shallots and crushed garlic and sauté for 10 minutes. Add the celery, juice from the remaining orange and cook on a slow heat for a further 10 minutes. Increase the heat and pour in the wine, adding the stock 5 minutes later. Once bubbling, reduce the heat and leave for 20 minutes, stirring occasionally. Combine the flour and water into a smooth paste and mix into the sauce, adding black pepper and salt to taste, stirring as you go. Remove the birds and drain the juices into the sauce. Place the correct side up on the roasting tin, drizzle with a shot of Cointreau and return to the oven at the same temperature for 10 minutes. Take the birds out and pour the sauce over them, then cover with foil and slow cook for 1 hour plus. Serve with mashed potatoes and greens.

My **dear friend Sally** gave me this recipe for a relaxed supper party. If your guest is late there is no need to fret, this delicious recipe will taste even better the longer it is left to slow roast.

GROUSE BREAST SALAD WITH RASP VINAIGRETTE BY GILLIAN MILLAR
(Serves 4)

4 oven ready young grouse
25g butter
2 tbsp. olive oil
Salad
100g raspberries
150g green beans (trimmed)
1 head chicory
Half a head of radicchio
Handful of small basil leaves
Handful of small mint leaves
50g whole blanched roasted almonds
Salt and pepper

DRESSING
3 tbsp. extra virgin olive oil
3 tbsp. ground nut oil
2 tbsp. raspberry vinegar

REMOVE THE BREASTS of the grouse (keep the carcass to use for stock another day). Heat the butter and oil in a frying pan until very hot, then season breasts with salt and pepper and place them into the pan and cook for 2 minutes on each side. Remove and place on a dish to rest, keeping them warm. Blanche the green beans for 30 seconds or until al dente, refresh in iced water then pat dry and halve. Trim the base of the chicory and separate the leaves. Tear the radicchio leaves into bite-sized pieces. Halve the raspberries. Put all the dressing ingredients into a jar, cover and shake the dressing until well mixed, then season.

Put all the salad ingredients into a mixing bowl and gently toss with the dressing, taking care not to bruise the raspberries. Divide between plates or put into a serving bowl, slice the grouse breasts and serve immediately.

I WAS DELIGHTED to receive this recipe. Gillian is the personal cook to the Duke and Duchess of Northumberland and I loved sampling her recipes. They have quickly become kitchen favourites.

OLD MAN'S WOODCOCK
(Serves 2)

GAME BIRDS

4 woodcock dressed
4 handfuls of red grapes
8 slices of Parma ham (finely sliced)
2 oz. butter
1 tbsp. olive oil or Oleifera
Cracked black pepper and sea salt

FILL EACH BIRD with a handful of grapes. Massage each bird with butter and then wrap them in Parma ham. Loosely cover and seal the birds in tin foil to allow the flavour to permeate throughout. Place in a roasting tin and cook on a high heat at 220°C {425°F} or the top AGA for 40 minutes. Remove from oven and open the parcels. Baste the birds with the juices, sprinkle with a little sea salt, open and roast for 40 minutes on medium heat 180–200°C {350–400°F}.

Once cooked, place the birds on a bed of watercress with all the juices—no sauces required! Serve with local potatoes and grilled tomatoes.

THIS MAN DOES NOT COOK; bless him he tries. His unconventional approach sometimes more closely resembles medieval weaponry than food, but this recipe works! Woodcock is extremely underestimated, yet it holds the most succulent and distinctive flavour. Try this one, even with frozen birds.

4 TUCK-IN PARTRIDGES
BY IRENE WHITTINGHAM
(SERVES 2)

4 plump partridges
1 ¼ lbs green grapes (seedless)
8 oz. streaky bacon
Juice of one large orange (or 2 medium)
½ tsp. of Provençal herbs
Black pepper and salt

GAME BIRDS

LINE A CASSEROLE DISH with long rashers of thin streaky bacon
allowing the ends to hangover the rim so that they can be used to
cover the birds later. Stuff each bird with as many grapes as you can fit
into the body cavity. Rub a little olive oil over each breast, add a good
pinch of salt and black pepper and finish with a sprinkling of Provençal
herbs. Pour over the orange juice and sit the birds on the bacon.

Fill in the spaces between the birds with any leftover grapes. Overlap
the birds with the bacon until they are completely covered. Tuck
everything in neatly and there you have your tuck-in partridge.
Cook in the oven at 160°C {320°F} for 45 minutes or until birds are
tender (this will depend on the age of the birds).

ANOTHER FANTASTIC RECIPE from my mother.

PAN-FRIED GROUSE BREASTS WITH SKIRLIE BY GILLIAN MILLAR (SERVES 4)

GAME BIRDS

4 young oven ready grouse
Olive oil
Skirlie
3 tbsp. olive oil
1 large onion (finely chopped)
Approx. 100g of oatmeal (optional)
Handful of pinhead oatmeal (optional)
Salt and pepper

SAUCE
300ml red wine
450ml grouse (or chicken) stock
1 tbsp. redcurrant jelly
25g unsalted butter (chilled and diced)

SEPARATE THE BREASTS from the grouse and remove the skin, then place in the fridge. Chop the carcass and make into a broth (as you would for chicken stock). Once you have the stock strained and seasoned, continue with the sauce (or use chicken stock if you are not making grouse stock).

For the sauce, put the red wine and the redcurrant jelly into a saucepan and reduce to about 2 tablespoons. Add the stock and boil, reducing by half and then season.

For the Skirlie, heat the oil in a frying pan, add the onion and fry slowly, stirring occasionally until evenly golden brown. Stir in enough medium oatmeal to absorb the fat, adding a handful of pinhead oatmeal for added texture (optional). Season with salt and pepper and continue to cook until oatmeal is slightly toasted. You may have to add a bit more oil if it is too dry. Keep it warm.

Take the breasts out of the fridge at least 30 minutes prior to cooking and season them with salt and pepper. Heat a heavy-based frying pan until hot and add 1 tablespoon of oil. Place the seasoned breasts in the pan and cook for 2 minutes on each side. Remove and rest in a warm place for about 10 minutes before slicing.

To finish, reheat the sauce and whisk in the chilled, diced butter. Do not boil. Place a spoonful of Skirlie in the middle of the plate and place 2 sliced grouse breasts on top and pour the sauce over them.

IT MAY SEEM EXTRAVAGANT using only the breasts, but the legs can be quite stringy and there is really no waste since the rest can be used for stock. Skirlie is a traditional Scottish stuffing, usually made with lard, but this is a healthier version!

A QUICK & EASY WAY TO COOK PHEASANT, PARTRIDGE OR GROUSE BREASTS
BY GILLIAN MILLAR

GAME BIRDS

SKIN THE BREASTS and place them in-between two sheets of cling film. Gently beat with a rolling pin and flatten to the thickness of a schnitzel. Coat in seasoned flour, beat an egg and pour over to seal. Finally, cover with breadcrumbs, then fry the breast and serve with a condiment like homemade tomato sauce.

RABBIT

RABBIT RECIPE BY ALISON BISHOPP
(Serves 3–4)

RABBIT

1 rabbit (jointed)
1 medium onion
2 or 3 carrots
1 garlic clove
1 bay leaf
Seasoning of choice
A little flour

BROWN THE RABBIT JOINTS in a little butter or oil, then set aside. Add the sliced onion to the pan and cook gently until soft. Add the carrots and chopped garlic to brown slightly. Sprinkle with a mean tablespoon of flour and stir well. Pour over enough chicken stock or water to cover the vegetables and stir until the sauce thickens, adding more liquid if necessary. Season to taste. Put the rabbit in a casserole dish with the bay leaf and cover with sauce. Cook in the oven at medium heat 180–200°C {350–400°F} for 1 hour. Serve with mashed potatoes and a green vegetables.

This will serve 3 or 4 people, but as there are only two of us, I use the leftovers—meat forelegs and ribs, along with some bacon or ham, a few mushrooms and some of the sauce—into a pie. The jointed rabbit can be marinated in cider with garlic and crushed juniper berries for at least 1 hour, then wiped dry, coated in flour and browned. The sauce is made with sliced onion, garlic and cider. Heat in the oven for 1 hour, adding a few sliced mushrooms for about 20 minutes before the end of cooking time. Sprinkle with chopped parsley.

M RS BISHOPP is one of my regular customers and she has been cooking rabbit since the War. Although not big fans of rabbit, my boys love this recipe.

EMMA'S RABBIT STEW WITH DUMPLINGS
(SERVES 4)

2 tbsp. Oleifera
450g diced rabbit
6 slices of diced streaky bacon (unsmoked)
2 red onions — finely diced
10 baby carrots
1 ½ pints of game or chicken stock
1 large glass of dry white wine
25g butter
25g plain flour
2 sprigs of fresh thyme
salt and pepper to taste

RABBIT

DUMPLINGS
225g self raising flour
110g suet
small handful of chopped parsley
chilled water — to bind
Good pinch of salt

USE A LARGE CASSEROLE DISH that can be transferred to the oven. Sauté the onions in oil on a medium heat till golden, add the bacon and rabbit. Stir for ten minutes till browned. Increase the heat to high and pour in the white wine, add the carrots then pour in the stock. Once bubbling reduce to a low heat for 30 minutes. Mix the butter and flour to a paste and add to the stew. Give it a good stir, season, add thyme sprigs and slow cook on the hob for one hour, covered.

Now for the Dumplings. Combine the flour, suet, salt and parsley. Use enough chilled water to make into a dough. Divide into 8 and roll into balls. Place the dumplings on top of the stew and transfer the dish to the oven 220°C {425°F} for 40 minutes till dumplings have doubled in size and are golden on top. Serve with local mashed potatoes and seasonal green vegetables.

SLOW COOKED RABBIT BY EMMA
(Serves 4)

RABBIT

2 whole dressed rabbits (ask your butcher to joint them)
8 shallots finely chopped
4 garlic cloves crushed
2 tbsp. Dijon mustard
2 tbsp. olive oil
300ml crème fraîche
A splosh of white wine

USE A CASSEROLE PAN that can be used on both the hob and in the oven. Heat the olive oil till sizzling, add shallots and garlic. Reduce heat and sauté till golden. Increase the heat for sealing the rabbit. Coat the joints with mustard and place on top of shallots and garlic until seared, keep turning them, this takes about 5 minutes, add a splosh of wine and place in a hot oven for 30 minutes. Give the rabbit a good stir and reduce to slow cook for 1 hour. Transfer to the hob, medium heat, add the crème fraîche and still until all the rabbit is coated and piping hot.

Serve with new potatoes, seasonal greens and a wedge of lemon.

VENISON

15 MINUTE MOIST VENISON LIVER
BY CYNTHIA SIDGWICK
(Serves 4)

VENISON

2 medium sized onions (finely sliced)
1 lb. venison liver
1 tsp. sunflower oil
1 tin of chopped tomatoes
1 beef stock cube
A dash of Lea & Perrins
¼ cup of water
2 tsp. Provençal herbs
Pinch of salt and pepper

SAUTÉ THE ONIONS in oil until golden. Portion the liver into
8 pieces and place on top of onions, cooking at medium heat for
4 minutes (2 minutes each side). Add tomatoes, beef stock cube, water,
Lea & Perrins, herbs and salt and pepper, then simmer for 10 minutes
and serve with local roasted seasonal vegetables or wild rice.

I WAS KINDLY INVITED to watch Cynthia cook this recipe a few weeks
ago. As luck would have it, her husband had returned successfully
from stalking earlier that day. This really is food on your doorstep
and I can honestly say I have never eaten such tender liver. Big thanks
to you both.

VENISON CASSEROLE BY EMMA
(SERVES 6)

VENISON

3 tbsp. olive oil
20 shallots
900g venison (diced)
400g button mushrooms
1 pint red wine
3 pints game/chicken stock
3 tsp. corn flour
1 tsp. gravy salt
2 tsp. cracked black pepper

ON HIGH HEAT place olive oil into a large casserole pan and add peeled, whole shallots. Shake pan for a couple of minutes until the shallots are lightly browned. Add the diced venison and stir until the meat is seared. Still on a high heat, pour in the wine and reduce to medium heat for 10 minutes, then add the stock. Remove from heat and add the button mushrooms. Cover and slow cook on either hob or oven for 1 hour. Mix the corn flour and water to make a smooth liquid paste and stir into casserole with the gravy, salt and cracked black pepper. Return to slow cook for 1 hour, remove lid, stir and continue to slow cook for another hour.

I LIKE TO COOK this the day before eating to let the flavours intensify. Serve with mashed potatoes, spring cabbage and Northumberland pudding, or perhaps I mean Yorkshire! Or why not try Game Chips (p34) as an alternative to mashed potatoes.

VENISON

VENISON CURRY BY DR. JACK LAMB
(Serves 6)

700g venison (diced)
4 tbsp. vegetable/sunflower oil
6 large white onions (finely diced)
2 red chillies (chopped)
2 green chilies (chopped)
10 cloves of garlic (chopped)
4 inches of ginger (grated)
1 cinnamon stick
8 whole cloves of garlic
8 cardamom pods
4 tsp. ground cumin
2 tsp. ground garam masala
2 tsp. ground fenugreek
2 tsp. ground asafoetida
2 cups water
2 tins chopped tomatoes
¾ block of creamed coconut
Handful of fresh coriander (chopped)

HEAT THE OIL in a heavy-bottom pan with the cinnamon stick, cloves, cardamom pods and green chilli. When hot add the onions, garlic, ginger and red chilli. Reduce the heat, add the ground spices and cook slowly until onions are soft and starting to caramelise. Now add the venison, tomatoes, water and creamed coconut. Cook on a low heat for 2 hours until venison is tender. Sprinkle the fresh coriander and serve with rice.

THE BEST CURRY I ever had! Thank you Dr. Lamb.

VENISON STEAK WITH CRÈME FRAÎCHE MUSHROOMS BY EMMA
(Serves 2)

VENISON

2 venison steaks
3 tbsp. olive oil or Oleifera
20 closed cup mushrooms
1 tsp. English mustard
6 tbsp. crème fraîche
2 good handfuls of watercress
Cracked black pepper
Pinch or two of salt

Place two tablespoons of olive oil in a large frying pan, add mushrooms and a pinch of salt and pepper. Cook on a medium to high heat for ten minutes until golden, then add crème fraîche and mustard and reduce to a low heat and stir. Take another frying pan and add 1 tablespoon of olive oil. The best way to cook these steaks is on a very high heat. Once the oil is sizzling, flash fry for 2 minutes on each side for medium rare and 3 for well done. Place on a bed of watercress, add the crème fraîche mushrooms and serve with crusty bread. All done in 20 minutes.

This is one of the easiest, yet most impressive ways to serve dinner in less than 30 minutes—quicker than Jamie Oliver himself!

ROASTED VENISON HAUNCH
BY ANN & JOHN JEFFREY

VENISON

1 large venison haunch on the bone (3–4 lbs.)
50g goose fat
4 garlic cloves (finely sliced)
2 tbsp. redcurrant jelly
Cracked black pepper and sea salt

GRAVY
1 ½ beef stock
1 tbsp. plain flour
2 generous glasses of red wine

PLACE THE HAUNCH in a good sized roasting tin. Slice shallow cuts
in the haunch and insert the garlic. Gently warm the goose fat and
coat the haunch. Season with cracked black pepper and a sprinkling
of sea salt. Cover in foil and roast on a high heat in the top AGA at
220–230°C {425–450°F} for 1 hour. Remove and baste the haunch,
then return to the oven with foil and cook on a medium heat at 180°C
{350°F} for 1 ½ hours. Remove from the oven and baste the meat,
then drain the juices (to be used for gravy). Coat with redcurrant jelly
and a sprinkling of sea salt then return to the oven on a high heat
for 40 minutes. Once removed, allow 20 minutes for the joint to rest
before carving.

FOR THE GRAVY, place the juices drained from the joint in a sauce
pan on a high heat. Gradually whisk in the flour, adding the stock
and wine. Once bubbling, reduce the heat to simmer for 20 minutes.
Season with cracked black pepper.

I SUGGEST SERVING the Jeffreys' haunch with local roast potatoes,
seasonal greens, carrots and border puddings—oh—I mean Yorkshire!
This is the perfect Sunday roast from one of my favourite couples.

SIDE DISHES

GAME CHIPS

4 large potatoes (local)
Vegetable oil for deep frying
Salt and pepper

PEEL THE POTATOES and slice as thinly as possible into rounds. Soak for 30 minutes in cold water to remove excess starch. Drain and dry thoroughly. Heat the fryer to 190°C {375°F} and fry for 3 to 4 minutes until golden brown. Cook in two batches to avoid sticking. Place on kitchen paper to remove excess oil. Sprinkle with salt and pepper to serve.

LEEK PUDDING
(SERVES 6)

8 oz. of self raising flour
4 oz. suet or vegetarian suet
2 leeks
Water for binding the pastry
Salt and cracked black pepper

MIX THE FLOUR, suet and a good pinch of salt. Slowly add the water to make a dough. Line a large size pudding bowl, and keep ¼ back for the top. You can roll the dough but it's just as easy using your hands. Slice the leeks and place in the lined pudding bowl, add the cracked pepper according to taste. Make the lid with the remaining dough and place on top. Completely seal the pudding in foil and steam for three hours.

PUDDING SUGGESTIONS

SIMPLE, EASY, QUICK AND LOCAL!

CHOCOLATE MOUSSE
(SERVES 6–8)

6 egg whites
3 egg yolks
1 large bar of dark chocolate
2 shots of brandy

SEPARATE THE EGGS. Place 3 egg yolks in a bowl and slowly whisk with the brandy (you can keep the 3 spare yolks for mayonnaise). Break up the chocolate and place into a heatproof bowl. Position on top of an almost simmering pan of water until melted, stirring occasionally. Refrain from letting the water over-boil, for it tends to ruin the chocolate. Whisk the egg whites until they are stiff, fold in the egg yolk mixture and then add the melted chocolate. Transfer to a pudding bowl or 8 individual pots, depending on your preference. Keep in the fridge. Best served with double cream.

SEASONAL FRUIT SALAD
(SERVES 6–8)

4 Punnets of mixed seasonal fruit
2 shots of kirsch
2 tbsp brown sugar
½ lemon

4 PUNNETS of Northumbrian seasonal fruit are needed for this recipe. As you can imagine, the list is endless depending on the seasons, but keep in mind most of the fruits freeze well. Why not try a good mix of raspberries, strawberries, brambles, redcurrants, blackcurrants and apples. Add 2 shots of Kirsch liquor, 1 tablespoon of brown sugar and half of a pressed lemon. Refrigerate for 2 hours before serving. Serve with local vanilla ice cream, I suggest chocolate or vanilla or local double cream.

PURLOINED MJ PUDDING
(Serves 6)

2 punnets of grapes OR 2 jars of preserved black cherries, drained
500ml Greek Yoghurt
500ml double cream
4 tbsp soft muscovado sugar

Cover the bottom of a medium sized quiche dish with either the grapes halved or cherries. Whip the cream until just thick and then combine the yoghurt. Completely cover the fruit then sprinkle the sugar on top. Place in the fridge for several hours or ideally over night. It must be uncovered to allow the sugar to form a hard crust.

A **Moore family** staple and favourite purloined from Debbie Phillipson many years ago.

NORTHUMBERLAND CHEESE COMPANY'S CHEESE BOARD

A **fantastic selection** of cheese; these are some of my favourites:

Elsdon
Chevington
Brinkburn
Cheviot
Reiver

Why not try this with local oat cakes, melba toast and the Mad Jam Woman's chutney. For those of you not yet clued in, Sandy's chutneys are available throughout Northumberland.

CONVERSION TABLES

WEIGHTS

IMPERIAL	METRIC
½ OZ	10 g
¾ OZ	20 g
1 OZ	25 g
1½ OZ	40 g
2 OZ	50 g
2½ OZ	60 g
3 OZ	75 g
4 OZ	110 g
4½ OZ	125 g
5 OZ	150 g
6 OZ	175 g
7 OZ	200 g
8 OZ	225 g
9 OZ	250 g
10 OZ	275 g
12 OZ	350 g
1 LB	450 g
1 LB 8 OZ	700 g
2 LB	900 g
3 LB	1.35 kg

DIMENSIONS

IMPERIAL	METRIC
⅛ INCH	3 mm
¼ INCH	5 mm
½ INCH	1 cm
¾ INCH	2 cm
1 INCH	2.5 cm
1¼ INCH	3 cm
1½ INCH	4 cm
1¾ INCH	4.5 cm
2 INCH	5 cm
2½ INCH	6 cm
3 INCH	7.5 cm
4 INCH	10 cm
5 INCH	13 cm
6 INCH	15 cm
7 INCH	18 cm
8 INCH	20 cm
9 INCH	23 cm
10 INCH	25.5 cm
12 INCH	30 cm

Oven Temperatures

GAS MARK	°F	°C
1	275°F	140°C
2	300°F	150°C
3	325°F	170°C
4	350°F	180°C
5	375°F	190°C
6	400°F	200°C
7	425°F	220°C
8	450°F	230°C
9	475°F	240°C

If using a fan oven you will need to reduce the oven temperature in a recipe by 20 degrees.

Volume

IMPERIAL	METRIC
2 FL OZ	55 ml
3 FL OZ	75 ml
5 FL OZ (¼ PINT)	150 ml
10 FL OZ (½ PINT)	275 ml
1 PINT	570 ml
1¼ PINT	725 ml
1¾ PINT	1 litre
2 PINT	1.2 litre
2½ PINT	1.5 litre
4 PINT	2.25 litres

American Cup Conversions

	AMERICAN	IMPERIAL	METRIC
	1 CUP FLOUR	5 OZ	150g
	1 CUP CASTER/GRANULATED SUGAR	8 OZ	225g
	1 CUP BROWN SUGAR	6 OZ	175g
	1 CUP BUTTER/MARGARINE/LARD	8 OZ	225g
	1 CUP SULTANAS/RAISINS	7 OZ	200g
	1 CUP CURRANTS	5 OZ	150g
	1 CUP GROUND ALMONDS	4 OZ	110g
	1 CUP GOLDEN SYRUP	12 OZ	350g
	1 CUP UNCOOKED RICE	7 OZ	200g
	1 STICK BUTTER	4 OZ	110g

GAME BY SEASON

THESE DATES will help you to know when and what is fresh and in season.

DEER SPECIES/SEX		ENGLAND/WALES/NORTHERN IRELAND
RED STAGS		August 1 – April 30
RED HINDS		November 1 – March 31
SILKA STAGS		August 1 – April 30
SILKA HINDS		November 1 – March 31
FALLOW BUCKS		August 1 – April 30
FALLOW DOES		November 1 – March 31
ROE BUCKS		April 1 – October 31
ROE DOES		November 1 – March 31

DEER SPECIES/SEX		SCOTLAND
RED STAGS		July 1 – October 20
RED HINDS		October 21 – February 15
SILKA STAGS		July 1 – October 20
SILKA HINDS		October 21 – February 15
FALLOW BUCKS		August 1 – April 30
FALLOW DOES		October 21 – February 15
ROE BUCKS		April 1 – October 20
ROE DOES		October 21 – March 31

Species	Great Britain
Pheasant	October 1 – February 1
Partridge	September 1 – February 1
Grouse	August 12 – December 10
Duck & Goose	September 1 – February 20
Woodcock	October 1 – January 31 (England/Wales/NI)
	September 1 – January 31 (Scotland)

WITH THANKS TO

OLEIFERA
PREMIUM COLD PRESSED RAPESEED OIL

Pilgrims
Coffee House

www.alnwickfoodfestival.co.uk

Game On Press